Leaf

Amanda Sullivan

NEWMAN SPRINGS PUBLISHING
320 Broad Street
Red Bank, NJ 07701

First originally published by Newman Springs Publishing 2023

ISBN 978-1-68498-940-9 (Paperback)
ISBN 978-1-68498-941-6 (Digital)

Printed in the United States of America

In memory of my beloved mom, who taught me how to dance in the rain, and my husband, for his endless love and support.

Many years ago in the winter landscape of Philadelphia, a baby girl was born. She was named Lynne Barbara after two dear friends of her parents. Lynne was petite, with sparse light blond hair and intense dark brown eyes.

She couldn't help it; that's just the way she was.

It did not take long for Lynne to be joined by a younger sister and two brothers. She naturally assumed the role of the ringleader, conducting her three younger siblings on many thrilling adventures and playful shenanigans.

She couldn't help it; that's just the way she was.

Lynne was often full of restless energy in school. In response to this, her teachers occasionally allowed her the incentive to read independently once her schoolwork was completed. She flourished in this autonomous environment that fostered her love for literature, setting her up to excel in school. Even though Lynne was not naturally extroverted, she quickly learned and mastered the skills of being approachable and making friends easily. She delighted in the opportunity to be helpful and a leader at school.

She couldn't help it; that's just the way she was.

Another passion of Lynne's was art. She drew throughout the day, whenever the opportunity presented itself. She created electrifying artwork with many different media. For Lynne, drawing and escaping into the world of art became a way of life, manipulating colors and shapes to creatively alter her backdrops. Lynne continued to have many interests such as writing, dancing, and swimming, but art was always her biggest love.

She couldn't help it; that's just the way she was.

Art soon became a career choice for Lynne when she decided to attend university to further develop her talents. Shortly after school began, Lynne met a graduate student with big brown eyes, dark wavy hair, and a warm smile. There was an instant attraction between the two. Michael was quiet and well-mannered. He was a talented potter who loved spending time hiking and camping. In many ways, Lynne was his opposite. Still petite, she was feisty, talkative, impatient, and despised camping.

She couldn't help it; that's just the way she was.

L.B.B

Regardless of these differences, Michael and Lynne were drawn to each other. They later shared their first kiss right after Lynne bit into an apple. Whether it was romantic or comical, this unplanned kiss set the tone for their relationship, and they were married within a couple of years. Their wedding was held on an exceptionally hot and humid summer day in a church that had no air conditioning. Lynne would vividly remember the bead of sweat that formed on the tip of Michael's nose and how it dangled there throughout the ceremony. She wore an elegant long designer gown with big framed glasses and bore a smile the entire time.

She couldn't help it; that's just the way she was.

After the wedding, Lynne and Michael settled happily into their new lives as a young married couple and moved to Nebraska. Lynne soon graduated and went on to teach art at a local high school. Being in a profession that allowed her to move around energetically suited her well. Lynne truly had a gift for teaching and helping students, catering to a diverse range of learning styles and abilities. She welcomed all into her rarely empty classroom, often becoming a safe haven for students.

She couldn't help it; that's just the way she was.

Not long after beginning her teaching career, Lynne and Michael had a son. Within a few years, two daughters completed the family. Lynne approached motherhood with the same enthusiasm and dedication as she did with all of her passions. From helping to design dance recital sets and leading clubs to cheering her kids on at concerts and performances, she was always involved. Lynne fed and watched over not only her own kids but also their friends and neighbors as well.

She couldn't help it; that's just the way she was.

Lynne stayed busy and never slowed down. She was an active member of the community and always appreciated the opportunity to make a difference. She remained devoted to both her own children as well as her students. When she witnessed multiple students struggle with severe personal hardships, she became a coordinator for the school's intervention program. Lynne personally helped students get their lives back together and on the right track, never giving up on them.

She couldn't help it; that's just the way she was.

Before long Lynne's three children were married with children of their own. Lynne cherished the role of being a playful grandma: babysitting as often as she could and hosting family dinners and trips. Spending time with her growing family brought Lynne infinite amounts of joy.

She couldn't help it; that's just the way she was.

After forty-two years of teaching, Lynne decided it was time to retire. She had big plans to spend additional time with her grandchildren, teach private art lessons, volunteer, and mentor. Sadly, none of her plans would come to fruition. When Lynne was nearing retirement, it was obvious something was not right. She started struggling to find the words she wanted to say when speaking. Lynne also began to no longer be her cheerful, upbeat self with infectious humor; instead, she became withdrawn and apathetic.

She couldn't help it; that's just what was happening.

Less than six months after her retirement, Lynne was diagnosed with frontotemporal dementia. Damage was occurring to her brain that caused problems in Lynne's language and behavior. The symptoms Lynne experienced continued to increase as the disease progressed rapidly. Lynne soon not only struggled to talk but started having a difficult time understanding what other people were saying as well. Those around Lynne began to notice her judgment had become impaired; her mannerisms and personality were different too. These changes were difficult for those around her to understand. Lynne was acting strangely and was even confused at times.

She couldn't help it; that's just what was happening.

Lynne continued to be surrounded by family and loved ones as her mind and body declined. Even though Lynne's grandchildren were often worried and scared by what was happening to their once lively and joyful grandma, they still wanted to visit. The family coped with her unpredictably worsening condition by uniting together. Michael was devastated by her deterioration but took meticulous care of his Leaf, the nickname he affectionately gave her when they first started dating all those many years ago. Lynne's children soon started to help support their dad and take care of their mom the way she had taken care of them and so many others. Lynne positively touched thousands of lives, creating an immense and immeasurable ripple effect. There is no way of knowing just how many people Lynne directly or indirectly impacted; the number is countless.

She couldn't help it; that's just what happened.

Conclusion

Lynne's husband and children attended to her strenuous needs through the final stages of her illness, along with the eventual assistance of a home health aide. Toward the end of Lynne's life, she was unable to speak at all and periodically struggled to chew or swallow. Her movements became stiff, and she eventually no longer recognized her loved ones. Less than five years after Lynne's diagnosis, she died at home, surrounded by love.

Pieces of Lynne continue to live on through her children; her passion for teaching has been carried on by her eldest daughter who teaches in the same school district. Lynne's energy and ability to theatrically share stories is illustrated in her son, and her desire to help others is demonstrated in her youngest child who chose a profession in social work and counseling. All six of Lynne's grand-children share some of her best traits including her artistic talent, her fashionable style, her sociable, cheery, and spirited ways, and even her same eyes.

Lynne lived life to the fullest. She was enthusiastically involved in grassroots organizations, committees, nonprofit agencies, and book clubs. She also wrote grants, was the art department chair at the high school she taught at, and sponsored student clubs. She met challenges head-on and always remained positive. Lynne was student-centered as a teacher, investing in everyone she taught. She had a talent for finding humor in tough situations and projecting an optimistic outlook; this remained true even after she learned of her diagnosis. Lynne had a vibrant and generous personality and was truly the person we aspire to be.

She couldn't help it; that's just the way she was.

Tips for Parents and Guardians

When a loved one is diagnosed with FTD it can be confusing and difficult to understand as well as scary for a child. As a caregiver or guardian it is beneficial to:

- Listen to your child, answer any questions honestly and age appropriately (in a way they understand), and provide comfort and reassurance. For example, for an older child: "grandpa has an illness in his brain called frontotemporal dementia. The disease will get worse over time, and there is no cure. We may see many changes in his behavior before he dies, but we will get through this together. You are not alone." Or for a younger child: "grandma's brain is really sick and it's not going to get better. Things will change, she may act or look different than she used to. It is okay if you do not understand what is happening. I will be here to help you."
- Offer a safe place for them to express their emotions by encouraging them to share, validating their emotions, and openly discussing how you are feeling, too. For example, "I hear that you feel really scared and confused about what is

happening to Uncle John. That makes sense. This is a hard time and I sometimes feel that way, too. All our feelings are okay to have."

- Children may find it difficult to verbalize their feelings: art, writing, music, creating crafts, and using sand or clay can help serve as outlets. Older children and teenagers can benefit from creating playlists of songs to help with various emotions they are coping with. Remember kids will process and grieve differently; there is no right or wrong way.

- Continue to follow a routine and if needed, provide warning of any potential disruptions to schedules. Creating and implementing new traditions to acknowledge your loved one can be beneficial, such as sharing a happy memory involving your loved one before bed to help keep their memory of them healthy, alive, and well.

- Permit your child to continue to see and interact with their loved one who is ill, preparing them as much as possible after changes have occurred so they know what to expect beforehand. Due to the manner in which FTD affects personality and judgment, supervision should occur on visits. It is okay if your child is feeling apprehensive or uncomfortable about visiting a loved one with FTD; do not force them to do so. Think of other ways your child can participate and help show love, such as drawing a picture, making a card, or a favorite recipe for their loved one.

- Continue to openly share memories of your loved one prior to their illness. Create a box full of tangible items such as photos, cards, and objects directly related to their loved one. You can also include written memories or stories.
- Increase your child's support system by allowing additional time with peers, friends, and family. Notify school, extracurricular activities, and church about what is happening.
- Make sure you, as the guardian, are also receiving appropriate support and assistance. Think of an oxygen mask on an airplane. You must secure your mask prior to assisting anyone else. Communities often offer various support groups for caregivers and grief/bereavement groups. Individual and group therapeutic services can also be helpful for processing and coping—for both children and adults.

Helpful Information

- Lynne was diagnosed with frontotemporal dementia (FTD) in October 2017. This type is the most common form of dementia for people under the age of sixty, despite being one of the less common types of dementia in general. It is caused by degeneration of the frontal and/or temporal lobes of the brain. It can also be referred to as frontotemporal lobar degeneration (FTLD).
- There are three subtypes of FTD:
  - Primary progressive aphasia, which includes three subtypes, is what Lynne was initially diagnosed with. PPA presents as an ongoing loss of communication: the ability to speak, read, write, and understand spoken language.
  - Behavior variant is categorized by noticeable alterations in personality and behavior, often occurring in people in their fifties and sixties, but can emerge in a person in their twenties or even in their eighties. Deterioration in decision-making, self-control, and a lack of empathy are often associated with this type.

- Movement disorders, neurologically based, can cause muscle weakness or wasting, stiffness, difficulty in movements, and deterioration of mobility. Language and thinking abilities can be impacted too. Progressive supranuclear palsy (PSP) is included in this category, which Lynne was eventually diagnosed with as well.
- Unlike Alzheimer's, FTD presents with a slow and ongoing, progressive deterioration in behavior, language, or movement. Memory will often remain reasonably intact until later stages. FTD typically affects people at a younger age with an onset ranging from twenty-one to eighty. Most cases are diagnosed between the ages of forty-five and sixty-four. Due to the younger age of manifestation, FTD has a considerably greater impact on work, family, and finances when compared to Alzheimer's.
- Unfortunately, much of the care cost is not covered by health insurance in the United States. The Association for Frontotemporal Degeneration posted the findings of a 2017 study funded and cowritten by AFTD and published in *Neurology*, stating that the economic burden of FTD is approximately $120,000 per year, nearly double the amount associated with Alzheimer's.
- FTD is also less known and recognizable compared to other forms of dementias. Many in the medical community remain unaware of the symptoms, and it is regularly misdiagnosed

as Alzheimer's, depression, Parkinson's disease, or a psychiatric condition. Currently, there is no cure or treatment to slow the progression of FTD.

For further information or ways to help, please visit the Association for Frontotemporal Degeneration at https://www.theaftd.org/

When someone whom you love is there but isn't,
we start by posing what we hope can be,
and then we're lost; who knows what must or mustn't
provide us light when it's too dark to see?

For one who's died, our tears can fill that chasm.
for death we understand, so we suppose.
but *present absence* is a cataclysm.
our heartstrings snap, catch any wind that blows.

When someone whom you love is there but isn't
because another now resides within,
take care; this mean imposter doesn't sicken
all that you knew of who and what and when

Hold tight to memories while still we live them
however frail and flawed they may appear.
for when they vanish, galaxies go with them,
and starless night encroaches with its fears.

When someone whom you love is there but isn't,
join hands with all or any who respond.
do what you can; there are no rules, no given.
it's love that's brought you here—and will go on.
for what it's worth,
for what it's cost,
no love is ever lost.

Written by Christopher Hershey
August 2018
For my brother, Michael, and my sister-in-law, Lynne Barbara

Sources

"About Frontotemporal Dementia: Types." Alzheimer's Association, 2022. https://www.alz.org/alzheimers-dementia/what-is-dementia/types-of-dementia/frontotemporal-dementia?utm_source=google&utm_medium=paidsearch&utm_campaign=google_grants&utm_content=types_of_dementia&gclid=EAIaIQobChMIhPCGwqDB9wIVSWxvB-B122A39EAAYAyAAEgK3qvD_BwE. Accessed May 2, 2022.

"Disease Overview: What is Frontotemporal Degeneration (FTD)?" The Association for Frontotemporal Degeneration, 2022. https://www.theaftd.org/what-is-ftd/disease-overview/. Accessed May 2, 2022.

"Nonfluent/Agrammatic PPA (Primary Progressive Aphasia)." AFTD, 2022. https://www.theaftd.org/what-is-ftd/primary-progressive-aphasia/nonfluent-agrammatic-ppa-nfvppa/. Accessed May 2, 2022.

About the Author

Mandy Sullivan, Lynne's youngest child, wrote this book after her mother became ill. Mandy struggled finding any children's books on this specific type of dementia for her own kids. She wanted to create a story that genuinely depicted the heartbreaking devastation of this disease, while also humanizing it and normalizing emotions of the individuals who are impacted by this experience. This story also serves to commemorate the life of such a cherished person. Mandy is a licensed independent mental health practitioner and certified master social worker with her own private practice in Nebraska. She specializes in therapy for children. Mandy assisted in Lynne's diagnosis as well as coordinated and managed her medical care.

www.ingramcontent.com/pod-product-compliance
Lightning Source LLC
Chambersburg PA
CBHW041052050726
47599CB00018B/2126